RASMUS MIKKELSEN

Middonaito Kurabu

Contents

1

The Origin of the Hashiriya

Starting in the 1950s, Japan experienced an economic boom. Citizens in Tokyo were more financially well off than ever, and much of Japan's population suddenly had extra money to spend. Motivated by Japan's cultural love for cars, many people began obtaining new vehicles. Some people bought cars for themselves, while other lucky individuals were gifted new cars by their wealthy parents. Cars such as the Nissan Skyline, Mazda Rx7, Toyota Supra, and other high-performance sports cars began to flood the roads of Japan. Unfortunately for the eager new car owners, bumper-to-bumper traffic infested main roadways due to the over eighty-two million cars being operated in Japan daily. This, of course, meant the owners of new sports cars rarely, if ever had the opportunity to test out their new cars. Faced with this dilemma, many of these drivers sought to find another way. They wanted to figure out a place and time when the roads would be open for recreational use. What better time than the late hours of the night, when the general working population had all gone to bed? And what better place than sixty-two kilometers of a brand new, smoothly paved highway?

The Metropolitan Expressway Bayshore Route, more affectionately known as the Wangan-sen became the new testing grounds and point of congregation for Japan's underground street racers. From this, the ones known as the hashiriya, the street racing and car modifying criminals of Japan's streets were born. Constructed in 1976, the Bayshore tollway route, locally known as the Wangan-sen became the epicenter of Japan's midnight car show and street racing scene. The mostly straight stretch of highway featuring underground tunnels and large bridges was perfect for the hashiriya racers to test their car's limits, specifically their maximum speed. This expressway, stretching from the Kanazawa ward of Yokohama to the city of Ichikawa in the Chiba Prefecture would see street racers speeding along its pavement nearly every night one after the other. In 1982 the official Wangan race was made and became the staple of street racing destinations. Adrenaline junkies racing modified cars along the Wangan often managed to exceed speeds of over two hundred forty kilometers per hour or two hundred fifty miles per hour. The hashiriya were rarely ever caught by authorities due to the lack of traffic cameras along the highway and Japanese police vehicles being limited to a top speed of only one hundred ten miles per hour or about one hundred seventy-seven kilometers per hour. With top speeds like that, police simply could not catch the street racers of the Wangan. After maintaining incredible speeds for over sixty-two kilometers, precisely steering around dozens of civilian cars, and easily evading the police, the hashiriya needed a place to stop and wind down. The Daikoku Docks were the perfect place for them. Daikoku, located in Yokohama Bay near the Wangan was a large public parking area and rest stop that anybody could visit and park their vehicle for free. everyone from high-end foreign exotic enthusiasts to bosozoku bikers would congregate at the large rest stop to show off their vehicles, admire others, organize races, and make new connections within the community. Police would often try to shut these car meets down, knowing that many of the cars at Daikoku were the same cars and drivers racing on the Wangan. The car meets shutdowns were desperate attempts by the Japanese police to disrupt the street racing events and maintain some semblance of power and control over the racers and hashiriya. Although the police were exercising their authority over all the hashiriya and related individuals, there was one group of racers police were specifically sending their message. This group was none other than the members of the Midnight Club, otherwise known as the Middonaito Kurabu, the most infamous and successful Japanese street racing syndicate in history.

2

The Midnight Club Speciall

Japan's car modifying and racing culture quickly gained massive popularity during the 1980s. The number of hashiriya grew exponentially every day, much to the distaste of the police and many civilians. Street racers were seen as reckless, arrogant, and a threat to civilian drivers, pedestrians, and public property. These beliefs about the racers were rather justified as it was far from uncommon for street racers to crash their vehicles while driving. These wrecks would at best injure the racers, damage their vehicles, and the roadways, or at worst injure or kill innocent civilians and bystanders and more. In large part, the hashiriya brushed these wrecks off and continued racing. Many would say that the wrecks were simply a byproduct of the street racing passion and that civilians simply ought to stay out of their way. One individual felt that there should be a different method though. A better and safer way. In 1987 a man named Eichii Yoshida-san joined forces with his partner and friend Kato-san. They, along with two more members founded a new racing club. Yoshida-san named himself the Chairman, elected Kato-san as the Vice Chairman, and decided the name of the club. Its name was the Middonaito Kurabu, otherwise known as the Midnight Club. The club member's ideology was to do just one thing, push their cars to their absolute limits and achieve maximum speed. They also had something few other clubs did, A code of ethics. The Midnight Club maintained and operated under a strict code of rules and ethics. The number one priority of all members had to be the safety of regular road users. If a member of the club displayed careless or reckless behavior while racing, they were immediately banished from the club. Members also had to maintain and respect the anonymity of fellow club members and were not allowed to disclaim their personal information either. The drivers of the club never went by their real names, opting for nicknames or code names instead, and could not speak of the club or their involvement with it to anyone. Midnight club racers rarely knew of the real names or lives of their fellow team drivers. The way club drivers raced was also very strictly managed. Members were allowed to race against each other in unofficial battles. This meant that these battles would not affect the driver's Win/Loss ratios nor give any of the drivers bragging rights or superiority over one another. The only time bragging rights, street cred, or Win/Loss ratios were affected was in official battles which occurred when members raced against rival club members and teams. Members were also expected to be professional while racing each other and especially rival club members. They were never allowed to act aggressively towards each other or rival team members and were to never drive in such a way that put their teammates or rivals in unnecessary danger when racing. They had to allow their car's performance and speed to do the talking. And the team drivers did exactly that. The drivers and cars of the midnight club quickly asserted their dominance on the Wangan speedway and became some of the most infamous and highly pedigreed racers and vehicles in the underground racing scene and the Wangan race. One of the most well-known of the members' cars was the Ishida special 930. Originally a stock Porsche 911 Turbo owned by Eichii Yoshida-san known as the Widowmaker, Yoshida-san spent an estimated two million dollars in the 1970s modifying his vehicle. Shipping his car to Germany and employing the expertise of Porsche's very own personnel, the technicians perfected Yoshida-san's car's aerodynamics, drivetrain, suspension, and braking systems. The Porsche technicians managed to increase the car's engine output to over seven hundred horsepower at the wheels. The 930's engine produced more power than a modern-day Porsche 911 GT 2-RS. These modifications made Yoshida-san's car one of the fastest cars to ever race on the Wangan. Alongside the Ishida special 930, members of the club drove highly modified Nissan Skylines, Mazda Rx7s, Honda Civics, Toyota Supras, and even other high-end performance vehicles including Ferraris and Lamborghinis.

These cars often cost the drivers millions of dollars. The members of the Midnight Club were oftentimes successful Japanese businessmen which were how these extravagant cars were afforded. The cars and drivers of the Midnight Club dominated the Wangan and quickly became the most formidable opponents to race against. Regularly achieving and maintaining over two hundred miles per hour for the entire fifteen-minute-long races on the Wangan was an incredible feat after all. To race at these speeds for such extended durations, the members' cars had to be incredibly well-built, reliable, and therefore often expensive. Although having an expensive and fast car was a large piece of the puzzle to dominating in the Wangan race and performing at the degree to which Midnight Club drivers operated, money, high-end cars, and fancy modifications only got drivers so far. To compete against Midnight Club drivers or consider attempting to become one of them, individuals must learn to harness elite-level driving skills, dedication, and discipline.

3

Getting In

As the Midnight Club's immense popularity and infamy grew, aspiring street racers flocked to try out for becoming members of the club. Although many aspired to become a member of the exclusive club, chances of being admitted were very slim with only about ten percent of applicants being accepted into the club, if the club was accepting new members in the first place. The number of members within the club rarely ever exceeded thirty members at any given time and the process to become a member was incredibly long and difficult. A well-modified, reliable, and fast car capable of safely maintaining at least one hundred sixty miles per hour or just over two hundred fifty-seven kilometers per hour for the entirety of the Wangan was required. This simple club rule weeded out a substantial portion of hopeful tryouts on its own. If you were wealthy or skilled enough to obtain a car that met the performance expectations of the Midnight Club, you were only one small step closer to getting in. When drivers tried out for the club, they had to race with one of the members. In the race, their skill and ability to drive safely and calmly at such high speeds were tested and judged harshly. If the members of the club felt that someone made one unsafe move, lacked confidence, or showed discomfort at any point in the drive, they were rejected. If the lead members of the club felt that you drove skillfully and safely enough to meet their standards, you were accepted into the final stage of application. Drivers were given a pink Midnight Club sticker for their car and named official apprentices of the Midnight Club. Now in the apprenticeship period or "Techi" as the members named it, individuals were required to attend every meeting, win races, and improve their driving skills over a minimum one-year period. If an apprentice missed even one meeting, did not win enough races, or did not show significant improvement over time, they were stripped of their apprenticeship and kicked out of the club. Although the mandatory length of apprenticeship was one year, the process often lasted up to five years. To make the challenging apprenticeship even more difficult, club meeting times and locations were not simple, nor easy to obtain. Due to Midnight Club members being wanted fugitives, club meeting times and location announcements had to take the form of coded messages, hidden within daily local newspapers. The meeting announcements were hidden within random ads and other inconspicuous sections of the newspaper. If drivers were able to overcome all these obstacles, they would finally become official

members of the Midnight Club.

New official members would be gifted the infamous white Midnight Club bumper sticker and were finally part of the most exclusive street racing syndicate in Japan. Knowing the extreme difficulties that come with attempting to be part of the Midnight Club, many hashiriya wanted to get the street cred of being a member without going through the hard process of becoming one. Ignorant drivers would simply buy or make fake white Midnight Club bumper stickers and windshield banners to pose as members of the club. The real members of the Midnight Club were understandably highly protective of their club's name and did not take kindly to posers. If a street racer placed a fake club sticker or banner on their car, they could certainly expect their vehicle to be severely vandalized at the bare minimum. Often, cars repping fake stickers were set on fire and burnt to their bare chassis. The Midnight Club did not tolerate posers and was more than happy to go to extreme lengths to maintain the club's image and integrity. After all the club cars and drivers always performed at peak performance and did not like the thought of posers tainting their public image.

4

Making History

Beginning in the mid-1980s, the Midnight Club and the high-powered vehicles dominated not just the world of street racing, but the world of top-speed record-setting and breaking. In 1985 the club claimed two-speed records. The first was set by a Porsche 930, achieving a speed of over two hundred ninety-eight kilometers per hour and the other was a Nissan S130Z that went over two hundred seventy-three kilometers per hour. Another Porsche 930 Turbo club car claimed one more record in the 1980s, achieving over three hundred two kilometers per hour in 1988. The next rest of the 1980s did not see any more records officially set by the Midnight Club or its vehicles, but the 1990s would prove to be incredibly eventful.

Starting in 1994, A Toyota Supra A70 achieved a speed of over three hundred twelve kilometers per hour, setting the bar very high for future records. The three hundred twelve kilometers per hour mark would not be broken again until 1995, but over the remainder of 1994 twelve more records would be set by various cars. Five records were set by Porsche Turbos, one of them achieving a speed of just over three hundred-eight kilometers per hour. The remainder of the records set in 1994 were set by a Honda NSX, three Nissan R32GTRs, a Mazda FD 3S, two Nissan Z32s, A Nissan S130Z, and a Ferrari 348TS. Eight more top-speed records were set by the end of 1995. The first car to break the three hundred kilometers per hour mark since 1994 was Nissan R32GTR, just barely achieving over three hundred kilometers per hour. The official speed it set was 300.21 km/h. After that, two Nissan R32GTRs managed to achieve two more records. One car achieved over three hundred eight kilometers per hour, and another set the highest speed record achieved as of 1995 with a speed of over three hundred twenty-one kilometers per hour. After that, a Porsche 930Turbo set a top speed of over three hundred-five kilometers per hour. By the end of 1995 two more vehicles, a Nissan R33GTR and a Porsche 964Turbo set top speeds of two hundred seventy-three and two hundred eighty kilometers per hour. No official records were set in 1996, but in 1997 four more records were set, one of which was the highest top speed ever officially achieved by A Midnight Club vehicle. A Nissan R32GTR achieved a speed of over three hundred fourteen kilometers per hour and two R33GTRs achieved top speeds of three hundred eleven and three hundred twenty-seven kilometers per hour. The final and high-top speed record officially set was a Porsche 964Turbo that set a top speed of over three hundred thirty-two kilometers per hour. This was and still is the fastest official top speed ever achieved by a Midnight Club car until the end of 1999. Top speed records were some of the most credited and widely known records of Midnight Club vehicles and their drivers. Records set by the Midnight Club did however include multiple more records of different types. Three lap speed time records have been set on the Tsukuba Circuit and club cars have placed at the top of multiple speed trials, most notably the Yatabe Highest Speed Trial. The racing performance and subsequent pedigree the Midnight Club drivers and cars developed were unmatched by any other racing team or group. They dominated almost every facet of speed in the street and track racing scene, and this did not go unnoticed for long.

5

Entering the Spotlight

Although the Midnight Club had begun as a secret underground street racing syndicate, the club rapidly rose to incredible fame in Japan. After the club became known across all of Japan, it was only a matter of time before the rest of the world would discover them too. By 1984 local news media became incredibly interested in the Middonaito Kurabu. A local magazine, Weekly Gendai Magazine published a special feature of Yoshida-san's 830 special in October of 1984. This feature came to be very popular among the public, and it sparked the public population's craving for more information on the Midnight Club. This boom in demand for more from Japan's population gained the interest of a growing magazine publisher, Option magazine. Option magazine saw the potential features and articles on the Midnight Club as their path to massive success in Japan. Fortunately for them, their beliefs were correct and success in Japan became reality for the publisher. Option automotive magazine published multiple features on the Midnight Club's cars and drivers starting in August of 1986, and they sold.

More and more features were published over the years and the club even got a feature in Option Magazine's 40th-anniversary issue. Other Magazines such as Best Car Magazine also jumped on the trend and published a feature in one of their June issues. Embraced by public news media and consumers, the members of the club did not shy away from features despite being targeted by Japanese police. The crew was getting features in Option magazine almost every other month and at one point and club members were showing up on local news, doing interviews, showing off their cars, and influencing the entire country. As the club's fame in news media grew international fame followed. The cars and members of the Midnight Club were featured in multiple British magazines, international news, and even on television. In 1990, Japanese manga artist Michiharu Kusunoki created the manga series "Wangan midnight" an animated series about street racing in Japan. This show was very clearly inspired by the Midnight Club and its member's cars. The show featured characters, vehicles, and locations that were directly inspired by the members of the club, their cars, and the locations in which they gathered and raced. This manga was highly popular and went on to do over forty volumes. Along with the manga, other shows, animated series, and even movie adaptions were created, directly inspired by the infamous street racers and their cars. The immense amount of interest in the Midnight Club paved the way for an entirely new culture and passion worldwide. For the first time in history, people in countries around the world were interested and passionate about Japanese cars and the car culture the country held. Car culture in countries like America was suddenly not entirely domestic. There was now a growing mass interest in not just JDM vehicles, but all imported and foreign vehicles. Other regions experienced this same spark of interest in imported vehicles all around the world and passion for Japanese cars and Japanese car culture specifically became a massive passion and interest worldwide. The Midnight Club was known worldwide by the 1990s and its fame was at an unprecedented scale. The club, its stories, and its fame were officially pressed deep into history. Although the Midnight Club was on top of the world of Japan's car culture and was basking in immense fame, Fate would soon take hold of the club and alter its future forever.

6

The War to End Street Racing

The Midnight Club dominated the streets around the Wangan and Daikoku for many years, but by the mid to late 90s, the Japanese police and government cracked down heavily on the hashiriya street racing. Legal restrictions and outright bans on the modification of all cars were put in place by the Japanese government and intensely enforced by the police. Utilizing the new legal leverage, police seized many modified vehicles, enforced dozens of roadblocks, and forced many hashiriya and street racing clubs to disband and stop racing. Car meets were regularly shut down by the police and drivers at the meets were often arrested for having a modified vehicle. Through the simple act of criminalizing car modifications, the Japanese government created a massive weapon against hashiriya and street racing.

The tensions within the car scene were exponentially heightened by the new war being waged against the entire scene by the police force and government. These circumstances forced many clubs, teams, individual drivers, and car enthusiasts into hiding; however, the Midnight Club accepted the new heightened risk and maintained its operations, still regularly racing on the Wangan. These operations continued until December 1999 when the story of Midnight Club's end began. On this cool December night, Midnight Club drivers were confronted by members of a rival Bosozoku biker gang while gathering at one of their usual meeting spots. The bosozoku bikers provoked the club drivers into accepting a race against them on the Wangan. With aggression from both the bikers and Middnight Club drivers, they set off onto the Wangan to start a battle. On the speedway, an aggressive turf war broke out, and drivers of both clubs drove aggressively and recklessly. One of the Bosozoku bikers lost control at high speed and caused a massive wreck. The wreck killed as many as seven to eight people, some bosozoku bikers, some midnight club members, but most importantly, multiple civilians. A wreck damaging teams' vehicles or even killing racers would be a horrible incident but would likely not provoke any major repercussions. The fact that civilians were injured and killed in this wreck meant the Midnight Club and its members had utterly failed at maintaining their number one rule. Their main rule of never endangering or harming civilians through their operations was harshly violated. This wreck marked the end of the Midnight Club. The very same night the crash happened the club was disbanded, and the kings of street racing were separated and sent into hiding along with so many other hashiriya and street racers. This is the story told by news outlets, internet forums, and most public media. There is something strange about this story though. This supposed crash in 1999 was very large and devastating, causing massive amounts of damage, injuries, and death, however, there is no evidence of a crash happening in 1999. There are no police reports, newspaper clippings, photos, or hospital reports proving this incident ever happened. The only source of information on this story is second-hand accounts and regurgitated stories. Many people were convinced by the story but dig a little deeper and some facts can be found in the fiction. Max power magazine, another successful and popular automotive magazine alongside Option magazine and others interviewed in 1996. This interview was with one of the top Japanese tuners of the time. During the interview, the tuner was asked how they felt about a recent street racing accident on the Wangan that had left seven innocent bystanders dead. His answer was along the lines of "eh, shit happens." The tuner did not have much worry about the incident or its repercussions. The details of this wreck seem eerily like the wreck described in the story of the Midnight Clubs' disbandment. An estimated seven people were killed, it occurred on the Wangan, and it was a street racing wreck that involved both cars and motorcycles.

It is theorized that this wreck was the incident described in the story of the Midnight Club's disbandment in 1999, however, this accident happened in 1995. So, when the club supposedly broke up in 1999, was it because of a break in its moral code or something different, and why do these two incidents sound so similar, despite occurring four years apart from each other? The 1995 incident may have been used as a cover story in 1999 to allow Midnight Club members to go into hiding. As mentioned previously, during the mid to late 1990s and especially in 1999, street racing and modifying cars became incredibly difficult to get away with. The situation of being at such a high risk of arrest for the club members was a daunting reality, especially as many of them lived their daytime lives as well-known wealthy businessmen. Using the cover story may have allowed the club members to avoid legal trouble, keep the police off their backs, and wait to resurface in the future. The information on the entire story and the real situation is limited and convoluted, however, one thing is certain. Accident or no accident, code or no code, the Midnight Club and its members never truly disappeared.

7

The Return of the Middonaito Kurabu

After the Midnight club and its members went into hiding in 1999, they were never officially seen in public for the rest of the 90s and early 2000s. Even though the club was formally disbanded it was still rumored that on some nights one or two of the Midnight club cars speeding down the Wangan could be heard and even possibly seen. Over the next two decades, throughout the 2000s and 2010s cars repping the infamous Midnight Club bumper sticker were seen multiple times. Cars were seen on various tracks at circuit speed trial events, car shows, and other automotive events. The legitimacy of the stickers and banners on the cars and the actual origins of the cars or drivers themselves were unknown. Regardless of their legitimacy though, the presentation of the bumper sticker on the cars proved that the love for the club and the presence of their influence still existed in all corners of the world. Other than these far and few sticker sightings and rumors of Club cars racing and appearing in car meets, the Midnight club cars and drivers were never seen nor heard from. That was until 2019 when something very unexpected happened. After the original chairman of the club, Yoshida Kato was arrested and faced legal troubles due to poor business practices and scamming business clients, he was

21

forced to resign from his position in the club. Tadao Tamura, the driver of a blue Mazda FD RX-7 became the new chairman of the club and made a profound announcement in an interesting way. Rather than taking an interview on a magazine or news channel, posting on social media, or any other more conventional methods, the chairman of the club opted for something different. A new website appeared on the internet, midnightracingteam.jp. On the site, there was a full page that wrote about the entire story of the Midnight Club, at least the history the members allowed to be published on the site. Along with that, the website contained a page documenting all the records the club vehicles achieved, a page detailing and timelining the history of the club, and even a contact and members-only page. On the records page, there were three records achieved in the 2000s. Two were achieved by a Mazda RX-7 FD3S, one in 2005 and the other in 2020. The third record was set by a Porsche GT3RS in 2021. These records proved that Midnight club cars and members did not disappear and were still racing and setting records. One piece of text on the website's "about midnight" page was incredibly significant. This website was not just a presentation of the story, history, and record accomplishments of the club but was an announcement of the club's official public return. At the bottom of the "About Midnight" page, there was a paragraph that stated the Midnight Club will return under the command of the new chairman. In addition, the street racing the club had engaged in so often previously will never be done again. Since the disbandment of the club in 1999 members of the team had found success in the professional racing world, developing sports vehicles for automobile manufacturers, setting records, and even running popular car modification shops. Considering these new successes and lives, the page claimed the members will no longer street race ever again. The Midnight Club and its drivers will only ever race on the track and will dominate from the shadows. Public appearances of the club members and their cars will be few and far apart from each other, but the ones who follow the club may rest assured that in every race they watch, every custom shop there is, and every bumper sticker they see, The Midnight Club just may be there. Along with the website an official Instagram account was created called midcarspeciall. The account posts beautiful photos of various cars repping the Midnight Club banner and sticker. Some photos feature cars mid-lap on tracks, some in car shows, and other photos depict the original club vehicles from the 1980s and 1990s. The account has amassed over forty-three thousand followers and has posted three hundred fifty-three times as of 2022. Something interesting about the Instagram account was the Accounts it follows. The midcarspeciall account only follows thirty-seven other accounts and although many of them are private accounts, some are public, and the cars featured in the account's posts are always repping the Midnight Club banner. For this reason, it is largely suspected by many theorists and Midnight Club fans that the accounts followed by the official account of the club are in fact members of the team or at least drivers closely related to it in some way. The Instagram page and website marked the beginning of a new era for the Midnight Club, and the future of the team is seemingly very bright. The spirit and presence of the Middonaito Kurabu will likely live on forever, not just through the incredible vehicles produced by the drivers or the digital accounts and pages, but through the culture, passion, and influence the most infamous street racing syndicate in history has created in millions of car enthusiasts around the world.